All About Color Blindness

A Guide to Color Vision Deficiency
for Kids (and Grown-ups Too)

Karen Rae Levine

Illustrated by Frank Walls

HALESITE
PRESS

HUNTINGTON, NY

For Andrew

Special thanks to Michael S. Loop, Ph.D.,
University of Alabama at Birmingham School of Optometry

Halesite Press LLC
PO Box 2011, Huntington, NY 11743
www.HalesitePress.com

Illustrated by Frank Walls
Cover Design and Technical Illustrations by Karen Rae Levine

Levine, Karen Rae.
   All about color blindness : a guide to Color Vision Deficiency for kids (and grown-ups too) / Karen Rae Levine ; illustrated by Frank Walls.

   p. : col. ill. ; cm.

   Previously published: Createspace, c2012.
   Summary: Corey, a fourth-grader, explains how his color deficiency caused problems in kindergarten and how he learned to cope with the special way he sees colors. Includes new and updated information on living with CVD and the science of CVD.
   Interest age level: 004-010.
   ISBN: 978-0-9885615-1-9 (hardcover)
   ISBN: 978-0-9885615-2-6 (pbk.)

   1. Color blindness in children--Juvenile literature. 2. Vision disorders. I. Walls, Frank. II. Title.

RE52 .L48 2013
617.759/0083

Foreword

Terrace Waggoner, OD

When my son T.J. was six years old, he came home from school with a note from the school nurse saying he was "colorblind."

Being an optometrist, I should have already known he had a color deficiency. I thought back to when T.J. was in pre-school and kindergarten. His teachers mentioned he was having difficulty learning concepts such as grouping same or different colored objects. I thought it was a learning or attention problem.

I didn't think it could be a visual problem because at age four, before he started pre-school, T.J. had been given a complete eye examination by a pediatric eye doctor who was a friend of mine.

I told my friend about the note from the school nurse. She confided that she didn't test the color vision of pre-school children because of time restraints and the difficulty of testing such a young age group. This is the case with most vision care professionals, and why I developed *Color Vision Testing Made Easy*.

I'm happy to say that *All About Color Blindness* will give children and parents alike the information they need to understand the basics of color vision.

Dr. Terrace Waggoner is one of the nation's leading experts on color vision, and he developed the first color vision test appropriate for young children. Dr. Waggoner and his son T.J. are now partners in the business of Color Vision Deficiency education and testing.

T.J. Waggoner, MA

Color vision played a big part in the education system when I was in elementary school and now color vision awareness is even more important. In many cases, smart boards have replaced chalkboards, which have been shown to be even more confusing to those who have Color Vision Deficiency (CVD). Folders are color-coded, behavior is marked by colored cards, and textbooks contain a profusion of colored graphs.

It's not uncommon for children with CVD to suffer a psychological backlash because, due to a fairly common physical deficit, they are repeatedly told that they are "wrong." It's very important that teachers, parents and students are aware and informed about CVD so that the millions of children with this condition can maintain their confidence and receive the best education possible.

Contents

Corey's Story

1

I have a red-green deficiency. That's the most common kind.

To me, reds and greens look more brown or gray. I can tell that a bright, shiny fire truck is red, but don't ask me to sort red, green and brown leaves. To me, they look like different shades of the same color.

4

Before I knew I had CVD, my color confusion could make me feel bad about myself.

In kindergarten, Mrs. Baker asked me to count the cherries on the tree.

I couldn't see any cherries at all.

I guessed, "Four."

No, Corey. There are six.

I thought I must not be very smart.

Then there was the time I drew a picture of my family. It looked great to me.
Look everyone. Corey's family is green. They must be from Mars!
Everyone was laughing.
Except me.

One day, my mom took me to an eye doctor. The doctor showed me pictures of different shapes made out of dots.

When we were done, the doctor told us about my color vision.

Now I understand!

I was glad my mom was relieved but it was a while before I understood it myself.

Since first grade I've been able to read the colors on crayons and markers.

For hearts and roses and cherries, I use colors called Red or Scarlet or Maroon.

For leaves and grass and turtles, I use colors called Green or Forest or Olive.

For people, I use colors called Tan or Peach or Brown.

But when I draw for myself, I pick colors that look good to **me**.

Millions of people, young and old, have CVD. They might need a little help sometimes, and have extra things to remember...

... but that's not a problem for kids with CVD because they're smart and fun and full of life, just like everyone else.

Color Vision Deficiency isn't the end of the world. It's just a different view of it!

Corey's Questions

Before you begin...

Pictures with this symbol are for readers who *do not have CVD*.

They are "de-colored" copies of pictures meant to help parents, teachers and friends know what it *might* be like to see the world with CVD.

These pictures are *approximations*.

CVD is as unique as the individual who has it.

Words in BOLD LETTERS can be found in the list of Definitions on page 25.

What is CVD?

CVD stands for Color Vision DEFICIENCY. CVD is a better name for Color Blindness.
People with CVD are not really colorblind. There are still many colors they can see.
Almost all colorblind children have a Red-Green DEFICIENCY.
They have trouble seeing shades of red or green or both.

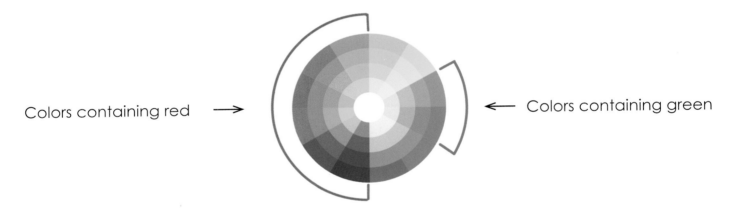

Colors containing red →   ← Colors containing green

There are also blue-yellow color deficiencies, but really only in adults, and usually because of medications or medical conditions.

Only in very RARE cases would a person with CVD see the world in shades of gray like a black and white movie.

How many people have CVD?

BOYS:

About one out of twelve boys has CVD.

GIRLS:

About one out of two hundred (200) girls has CVD.

How do I know if I have CVD?

Testing for CVD is as easy as looking at pictures. Shapes or numbers are drawn among a pattern of colored dots. Someone with a red-green deficiency will not be able to make out green shapes on a red background or red shapes on a green background.

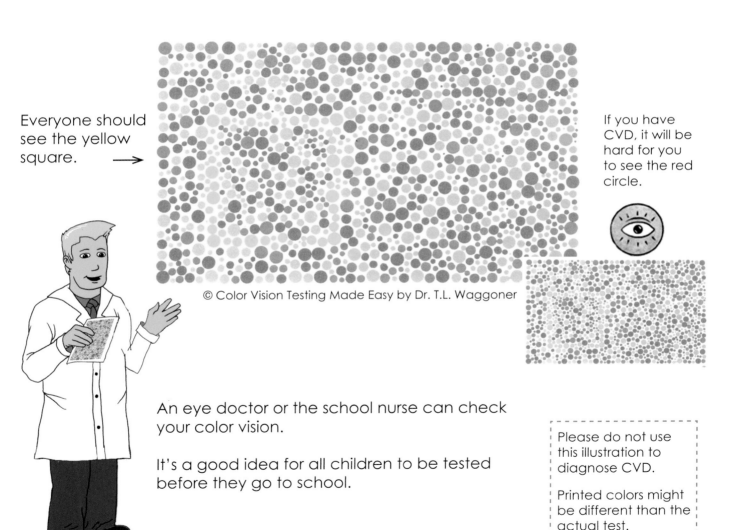

Everyone should see the yellow square. →

If you have CVD, it will be hard for you to see the red circle.

© Color Vision Testing Made Easy by Dr. T.L. Waggoner

An eye doctor or the school nurse can check your color vision.

It's a good idea for all children to be tested before they go to school.

Please do not use this illustration to diagnose CVD.

Printed colors might be different than the actual test.

17

What do people with CVD see?

To a person with a red-green color DEFICIENCY, shades of red or green look more brown or tan, or sometimes even black. For many, red and green look alike.

Colors that use a combination of red could also look different.
If you couldn't see the red part of purple,
it would look like blue.

Orange would look more like yellow or gold.

Oranges or
grapefruits?

Lighting makes a difference too.
Colors are always more visible in
brighter light.

Living with CVD

The best thing you can do if you have CVD is to be AWARE of it. Know that it's not a SERIOUS condition and be PATIENT with people who don't understand.

If you have CVD, it's important to remember that your vision has nothing to do with how smart you are.

If the colors are confusing, just say so!

What can I do at school?

Some examples of school assignments that can be confusing:

- Color names

- Math problems that use color (like patterns and counting)

- Art assignments that require certain colors (like rainbows and traffic lights)

- Map reading

- Charts and graphs

- Biology, Geology and Chemistry experiments

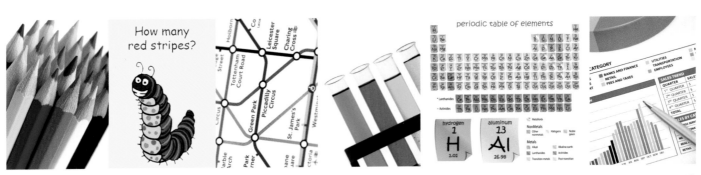

It helps to:

- Label your art supplies.
- Remember color names for objects that are used often (like hearts and grass).
- Become familiar with color names.

Here is a chart of **COLOR GROUPS** and the names of some of the colors in each group.

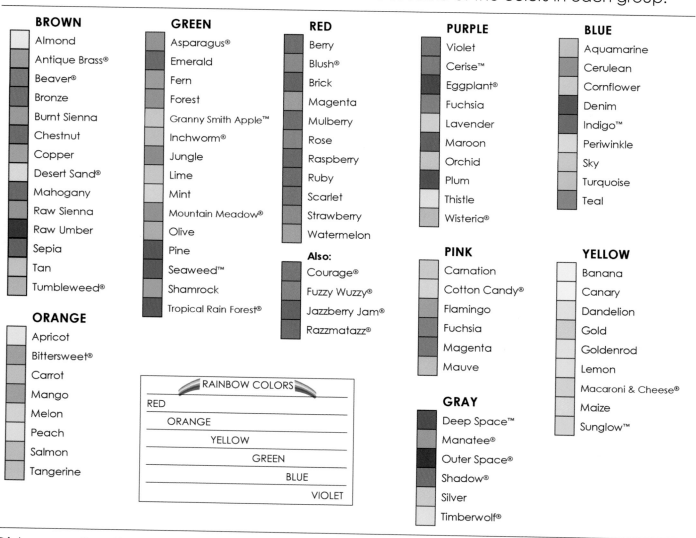

BROWN
Almond
Antique Brass®
Beaver®
Bronze
Burnt Sienna
Chestnut
Copper
Desert Sand®
Mahogany
Raw Sienna
Raw Umber
Sepia
Tan
Tumbleweed®

ORANGE
Apricot
Bittersweet®
Carrot
Mango
Melon
Peach
Salmon
Tangerine

GREEN
Asparagus®
Emerald
Fern
Forest
Granny Smith Apple™
Inchworm®
Jungle
Lime
Mint
Mountain Meadow®
Olive
Pine
Seaweed™
Shamrock
Tropical Rain Forest®

RED
Berry
Blush®
Brick
Magenta
Mulberry
Rose
Raspberry
Ruby
Scarlet
Strawberry
Watermelon

Also:
Courage®
Fuzzy Wuzzy®
Jazzberry Jam®
Razzmatazz®

PURPLE
Violet
Cerise™
Eggplant®
Fuchsia
Lavender
Maroon
Orchid
Plum
Thistle
Wisteria®

PINK
Carnation
Cotton Candy®
Flamingo
Fuchsia
Magenta
Mauve

GRAY
Deep Space™
Manatee®
Outer Space®
Shadow®
Silver
Timberwolf®

BLUE
Aquamarine
Cerulean
Cornflower
Denim
Indigo™
Periwinkle
Sky
Turquoise
Teal

YELLOW
Banana
Canary
Dandelion
Gold
Goldenrod
Lemon
Macaroni & Cheese®
Maize
Sunglow™

RAINBOW COLORS
RED
ORANGE
YELLOW
GREEN
BLUE
VIOLET

Did you notice that many colors have the same name as the object they describe?

What can I do at home?

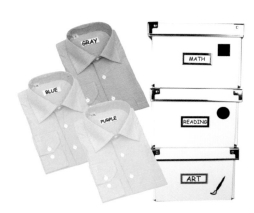

- Let your family know when colors are confusing.
- Set up a system to match your clothes.
- Be creative with ways to organize without using colors, like using words or shapes.
- Use all the tools you've already been using!

What can I do at play?

- Board games and video games are usually very colorful. Find the ones you like to play and don't worry about the games that frustrate you.
- Playing fields and gym courts are full of color-coded boundary lines. Sometimes it might be hard to tell one team uniform from the other. If any of this is a problem, explain your color confusion to your coach.
- Art projects are fun and you can create them with colors you like. It just has to look good to you! (There are many artists with CVD, including the illustrator of this book.)

What can I do everywhere I go?

- Trust yourself.
- Be polite.
- Remember that CVD isn't the end of the world...it's just a different view of it!

The Science of CVD

How is CVD inherited?

In children, CVD is almost always INHERITED.

CVD is a TRAIT passed down from parents to children.

- Women can be CARRIERS of the TRAIT without actually having CVD themselves.
- For a boy to have CVD, his mom must either have CVD or be a CVD CARRIER.
- For a girl to have CVD, the TRAIT must be present in both her mom and her dad.

Here is a chart showing the possibilities for a boy or a girl to INHERIT CVD, or for a girl to be a CVD CARRIER, based on their parents' CVD TRAITS.

Will their...	*Carrier Mom*	*CVD Mom*	*CVD Dad*	*CVD Dad Carrier Mom*	*CVD Dad CVD Mom*
...son have CVD?	50% CHANCE	YES	NO	50% CHANCE	YES
...daughter have CVD?	NO	NO	NO	50% CHANCE	YES
...daughter be a CARRIER?	50% CHANCE	YES	YES	YES	YES

How does the brain see colors?

The eye is the home of millions of NERVE CELLS that collect bits and pieces of information about what we see.

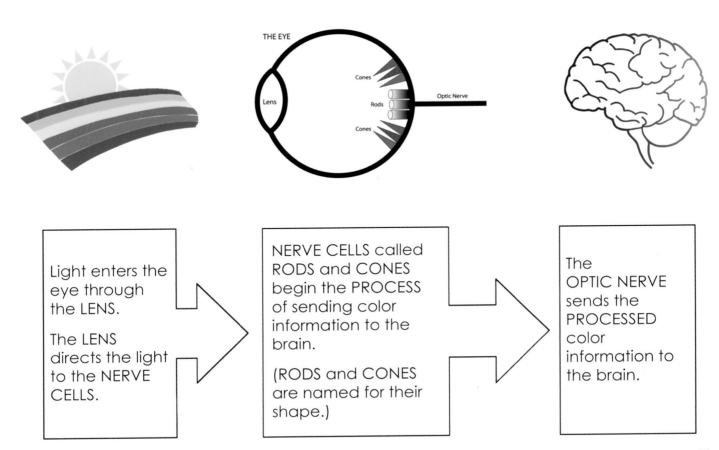

THE EYE

Cones

Lens

Rods

Optic Nerve

Cones

Light enters the eye through the LENS.

The LENS directs the light to the NERVE CELLS.

NERVE CELLS called RODS and CONES begin the PROCESS of sending color information to the brain.

(RODS and CONES are named for their shape.)

The OPTIC NERVE sends the PROCESSED color information to the brain.

How do rods and cones work?

RODS and CONES break down every color we see and then the brain puts them back together.

For example, let's pick a color from the rainbow picture on the previous page:

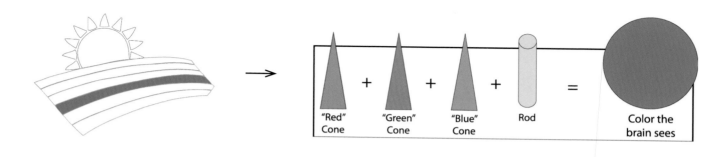

RODS only recognize black and white and shades of gray. (They help us see in dim light.)
Three different kinds of CONES recognize reds and greens and blues.
People who have CVD have CONES (red or green or both) that don't work properly.
The brain gets an incomplete or DEFICIENT color package.

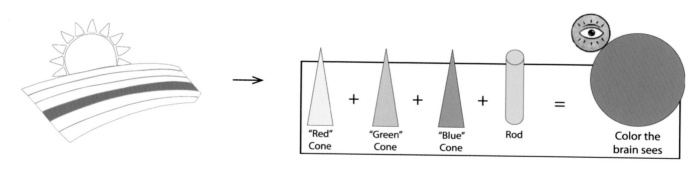

Definitions

Found on page:

For Parents and Teachers

In the U.S., some states require color vision testing for elementary school children. Unfortunately, there is nothing mandated beyond that. At best, parents are given a form letter containing the cryptic word "colorblind," and teachers are left completely out of the loop. The disappointing consensus is that "it doesn't matter because there is no cure." There might not be a cure, but it certainly does matter.

Think of a young child with CVD. Even before entering kindergarten, how many times has he (or she) already been told he was wrong when he chose a color or completed a pattern or moved to a space on a game board? A child with CVD has no frame of reference to say, "Maybe I can't see that color," or "Maybe those are different colors that look the same to me." A child's natural reaction would be, "I must not be smart enough to know that."

For fear of ridicule or admonishment, children with CVD tend to keep their color confusion to themselves. Parents and teachers can easily interpret the color "mistakes" of these children as a learning disability, an attention disorder, or even anti-social behavior.

The result is a child with diminished self-confidence, whose learning opportunities are hindered by lessons that rely on color association. The solution is deceptively easy: AWARENESS.

Parents:

- If you suspect that your child has CVD, have him or her evaluated by a professional with a color vision test that is age-appropriate.

- If your child has CVD, don't let anyone tell you it doesn't matter!

- Learn about and understand your child's color confusion.

- Communicate with your child honestly and matter-of-factly.

- Create a collaborative dialogue with your child's community of teachers.

- At some point, you can guide your child concerning career choices. Some occupations require color proficiency. (More detailed information can be found in the "Parents" section of www.AllAboutColorBlindness.com.)

Teachers can help by:

- Labeling art materials as well as classroom guides like folders, shelves and cubbies.

- Avoiding or modifying lessons and assignments that rely on color coding or color recognition.

- Avoiding colored chalk (especially difficult to see on a green board).

- Assigning partners for science experiments and map reading.

- Flagging color-dependent questions on standardized tests.

- Understanding and respecting children with Color Vision Deficiency.

Resources

www.AllAboutColorBlindness.com

The companion site for this book, including updated and expanded information, special downloads and even more helpful links.

www.TestingColorVision.com

Includes advice for parents and teachers and also practical coping techniques for children. A color vision test appropriate for preschoolers can be purchased here.

www.AllAboutVision.com

A comprehensive, up-to-date consumer resource about all aspects of eye health and vision correction.

www.ColourBlindAwareness.org

A UK based organization founded to raise awareness of color blindness and to support colorblind people and their friends and families.

www.colblindor.com

Color vision essentials: facts, articles, tests and tools.

About the Author

Karen Rae Levine, the mother of a bright and vibrant son with CVD, has been a long-time advocate for CVD awareness. A former aerospace engineer, software manager and graphic designer, she returned to her childhood love of writing and earned an MFA in Creative Writing from The New School in Manhattan. Years in the making, *All About Color Blindness* has been a labor of love.

Author website: www.KarenRaeLevine.com

ATTENTION PARENTS, EDUCATORS AND HEALTH PROFESSIONALS
Karen speaks to groups who want to discover more about coping with CVD.

- Health, eduction and library conferences
- School Board, PTA and faculty meetings
- School classrooms or assemblies

For more detailed Information or to schedule a talk or workshop, go to:

www.AllAboutColorBlindness.com

About the Illustrator

Frank Walls has a BFA in Illustration from the Cleveland Institute of Art. Working in the book and board game industries, Frank is an artist and designer who has CVD.